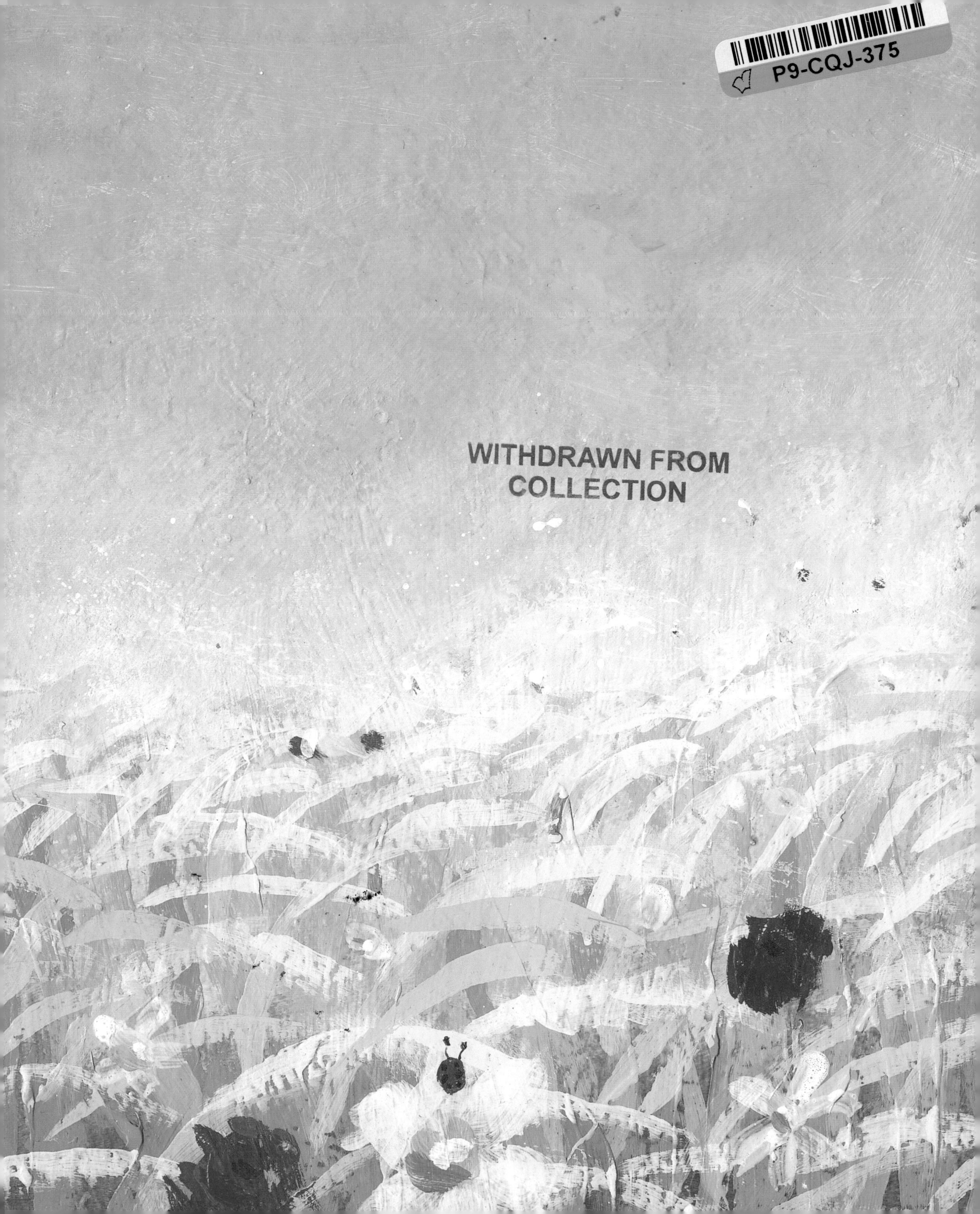

Over on the Farm

A COUNTING PICTURE BOOK RHYME

By Christopher Gunson

Scholastic Press

New York

Library of Congress Cataloging-in-Publication Data

Gunson, Christopher.
Over on the farm : a counting picture book rhyme / Christopher Gunson.
p. cm.
Summary: Mother animals instruct their little ones to stretch, scratch, or snuggle
as the reader counts the babies while wandering through farm, forest, and fields.
ISBN 0-590-13445-0
[1. Mother and child—Fiction. 2. Animals—Fiction.
3. Counting. 4. Stories in rhyme.]   I. Title
PZ8.3.G9580v   1997
[E]—dc20
95-25929
CIP
AC
12 11 10 9 8 7 6 5 4 3 2 1   7 8 9/9 0 0/1 0/2
Printed in Singapore   46
First Scholastic printing, April 1997
The text type was set in 20 point Stone Informal.
Book design by Edward Miller

For N.G.

Over on the farm in the early morning sun
lived a clever mother cat
and her little cat one.

"Stretch," said the mother.
"I stretch," said the one.

So he stretched and felt warm
in the early morning sun.

Over in the field in the green and the blue
lived a woolly mother sheep
and her little sheep two.

"Leap," said the mother.
"We leap," said the two.

So they both leapt together
in the green and the blue.

Over in the pond by an old willow tree
lived a happy mother frog
and her little froggies three.

"Splash," said the mother.
"We splash," said the three.

So they splashed and they sploshed
by the old willow tree.

Over in the forest on an oak leaf floor
lived a sly mother fox
and her little foxes four.

"Rustle," said the mother.
"We rustle," said the four.

So they rustled and they rolled
on the oak leaf floor.

Over on the hill by a buzzy beehive
lived a fluffy mother rabbit
and her little rabbits five.

"Hop," said the mother.
"We hop," said the five.

So they hopped and they jumped
by the buzzy beehive.

Over in the wood in a nest made of sticks
lived a wise mother owl
and her little owls six.

"Blink," said the mother.
"We blink," said the six.

So they blinked in the sunlight
in the nest made of sticks.

Over in the orchard by a hut old and wooden
lived a fussy mother hen
and her little chicks seven.

"Scratch," said the mother.
"We scratch," said the seven.

So they scratched and they pecked
by the hut old and wooden.

Over on the river in the rushes tall and straight
lived a proud mother duck
and her little ducks eight.

"Paddle," said the mother.
"We paddle," said the eight.

So they paddled in and out
of the rushes tall and straight.

Over in the garden by a windy washing line
lived a chirpy mother bird
and her little birdies nine.

"Flap," said the mother.
"We flap," said the nine.

So they flapped and they cheeped
by the windy washing line.

Over on the farm in a warm muddy pen
lived a kind mother pig
and her little piggies ten.

"Snuggle," said the mother.
"We snuggle," said the ten.

So they snuggled and they slept
in their warm muddy pen.

one

two

three

four

five

six

seven

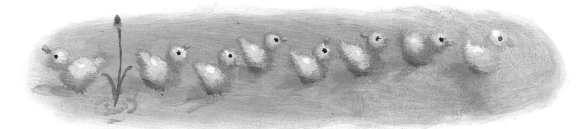

eight

nine

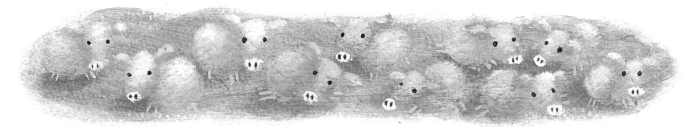

ten